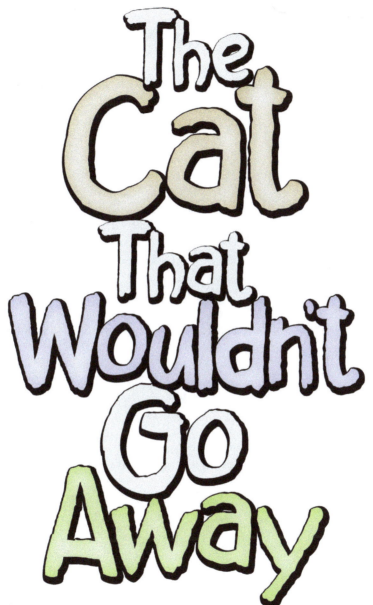

The Cat That Wouldn't Go Away

Rianna Facey & Tywanna Gardner

Copyright © 2018 Rianna Facey & TyWanna Gardner.

Illustrations by Noah Ray

All rights reserved. No part of this book may be used or reproduced by any means, graphic, electronic, or mechanical, including photocopying, recording, taping or by any information storage retrieval system without the written permission of the author except in the case of brief quotations embodied in critical articles and reviews.

This book is a work of non-fiction. Unless otherwise noted, the author and the publisher make no explicit guarantees as to the accuracy of the information contained in this book and in some cases, names of people and places have been altered to protect their privacy.

WestBow Press books may be ordered through booksellers or by contacting:

WestBow Press
A Division of Thomas Nelson & Zondervan
1663 Liberty Drive
Bloomington, IN 47403
www.westbowpress.com
1 (866) 928-1240

Because of the dynamic nature of the internet, any web addresses or links contained in this book may have changed since publication and may no longer be valid. The views expressed in this work are solely those of the author and do not necessarily reflect the views of the publisher, and the publisher hereby disclaims any responsibility for them.

Any people depicted in stock imagery provided by Thinkstock are models, and such images are being used for illustrative purposes only. Certain stock imagery © Thinkstock.

ISBN: 978-1-9736-1668-9 (sc)
ISBN: 978-1-9736-1669-6 (e)

Library of Congress Control Number: 2018900454

Print information available on the last page.

WestBow Press rev. date: 1/19/2018

The Cat That Wouldn't Go Away

Have you ever met a cat that wouldn't go away? i did. it was the middle of May when a cat showed up on my porch one day.

i asked my mom what he wanted and why he was there. She thought that he must be lost and belonged to one of the neighbors.

i thought the cat was looking for toys so i ran up to my room and brought him down toys.

He sniffed them and walked away.

What's wrong with this cat? Who doesn't like toys, i asked?
A neighbor nearby said, "He's hungry. He's looking for food."

My mom went to the store and bought food for the cat. A man working in the area said, "Now he'll never go away." The cat ate the food like he hadn't eaten in months.

Day after day he walked me to the car. He walked me to the house. i thought that he would walk me to a little mouse.

One day my mom saw the cat being bullied by larger cats.

They surrounded him. One cat ran towards him and knocked him into the street.

The little cat ran away. He didn't give up though. He came back another day. it's August now and the cat is still here. He won't go away so i guess he'll stay.

"if you meet a cat that won't go away i hope your cat is friendly."

About the Author

Rianna Facey is an eight year old girl that loves to dance, write, and talk. Rianna is a third grader at Calvin Rodwell Elementary School in Baltimore City. She plays tennis at an after school program where she attends school. In August 2017 her team won the City Wide Championship for schools at the US Open. Rianna enjoys attending church services and is a member of Concord Baptist Church in Baltimore, Maryland. In her spare time she takes gymnastic classes at Thrive in Annapolis, Maryland. Rianna will engage anyone in conversation if given the chance no matter their age.

CPSIA information can be obtained
at www.ICGtesting.com
Printed in the USA
BVHW021207250522
638070BV00015B/181